—MONSTERS DO MATH!—

MUMMIES MULTIPLY!

BY THERESE M. SHEA

Gareth Stevens PUBLISHING

Please visit our website, www.garethstevens.com. For a free color catalog of all our high-quality books, call toll free 1-800-542-2595 or fax 1-877-542-2596.

Cataloging-in-Publication Data

Names: Shea, Therese M.
Title: Mummies multiply! / Therese M. Shea.
Description: New York : Gareth Stevens Publishing, 2019. | Series: Monsters do math! | Includes glossary and index.
Identifiers: LCCN ISBN 9781538232989 (pbk.) | ISBN 9781538229347 (library bound) | ISBN 9781538232996 (6 pack)
Subjects: LCSH: Multiplication--Juvenile literature. | Arithmetic--Juvenile literature. | Mummies--Juvenile literature.
Classification: LCC QA115.S54 2019 | DDC 513.2'13--dc23

First Edition

Published in 2019 by
Gareth Stevens Publishing
111 East 14th Street, Suite 349
New York, NY 10003

Designer: Sarah Liddell
Editor: Kate Light
Illustrator: Bobby Griffiths

Photo credits: p. 4 Nyrok555/Shutterstock.com; p. 5 Fer Gregory/Shutterstock.com; p. 7 Andrea Izzotti/Shutterstock.com; p. 8 eldeiv/Shutterstock.com; p. 10 Photo 12/Contributor/Universal Images Group/Getty Images; p. 12 Science & Society Picture Library/Contributor/SSPL/Getty Images; p. 15 Danita Delmont/Shutterstock.com; p. 16 DEA PICTURE LIBRARY/Contributor/De Agostini/Getty Images; p. 18 Denis Burdin/Shutterstock.com; p. 20 Kekyalyaynen/Shutterstock.com; p. 21 PHAS/Contributor/Universal Images Group/Getty Images.

Printed in the United States of America

CPSIA compliance information: Batch #CW19GS: For further information contact Gareth Stevens, New York, New York at 1-800-542-2595.

CONTENTS

Words in the glossary appear in **bold** type the first time they are used in the text.

MONSTER MUMMIES?

An ancient tomb, or burial room, has been discovered. **Archaeologists** force open a door, and out walks . . . a mummy! This would be pretty scary, wouldn't it? But what if you could ask the mummy for help with your math homework—and it was good at it?

The mummies in this book are really good at multiplication. They'll help you understand what multiplication means and offer some tips for making it easier. Check your answers to the problems in the answer key on page 22.

MUMMIES AREN'T JUST MAKE-BELIEVE. A MUMMY IS ANY DEAD BODY THAT'S BEEN **PRESERVED**, EITHER BY NATURE OR BY HUMANS.

MUMMIES IN LINE

A group of mummies might be scary—and hard to count, too! If they lined up in rows and columns, their number would be much easier to figure out. This is called an array.

Imagine you opened a tomb and saw 5 rows with 7 mummies each walking toward you! You could count each mummy, or you could add the 5 rows like this:

$$7 + 7 + 7 + 7 + 7$$

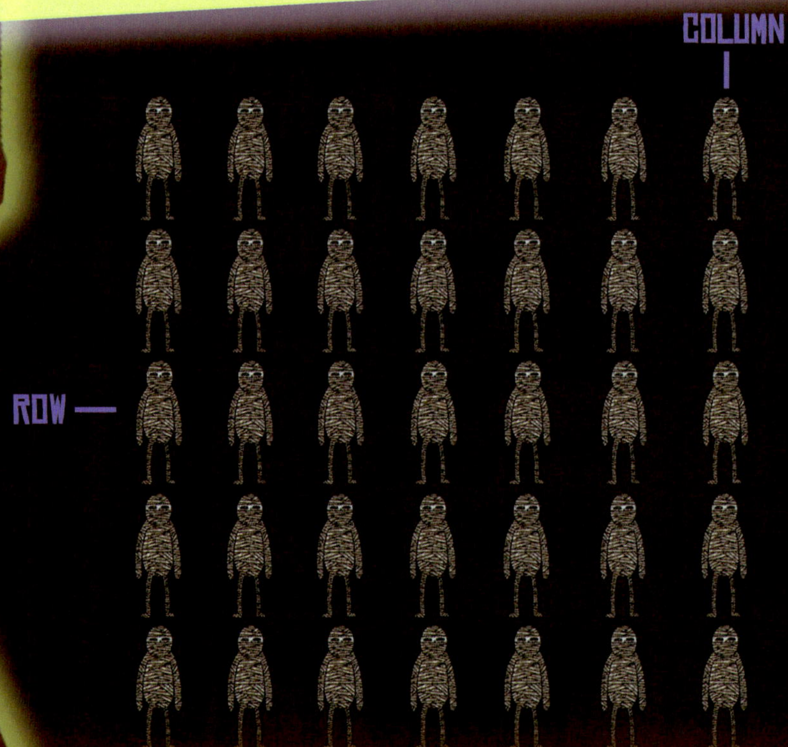

You can multiply the number of rows by the number of mummies in each row. The product, or answer, is the total number of mummies.

5 rows x 7 mummies in each row = ? mummies

If you know your multiplication facts, the second method is easier!

MONSTER FACTS!

ANCIENT EGYPTIANS MADE MUMMIES BY REMOVING PARTS FROM INSIDE DEAD BODIES. THEN, THEY CLEANED THE BODIES AND LET THEM DRY. FINALLY, THE BODIES WERE RUBBED WITH MATTER TO PRESERVE THEM AND WRAPPED IN CLOTH.

CANOPIC JARS

MONSTER FACTS!

WHEN MAKING MUMMIES, ANCIENT EGYPTIANS TOOK THE BRAIN OUT THROUGH THE NOSE WITH A HOOK! SOME BODY PARTS WERE PLACED IN SPECIAL CONTAINERS CALLED CANOPIC [KAH-NOH-PIHK] JARS.

A number of bodies are being prepared to be mummified. They are laid out in rows of equal number. How many bodies will be made into mummies?

Use the array to help you write a multiplication sentence. Then, solve it.

Hint: It doesn't matter which **factor** comes first in a multiplication sentence. The product is the same!

BEWARE, THIEVES!

MONSTER FACTS!

IN SCARY MOVIES, MUMMIES COME ALIVE TO GET REVENGE AGAINST PEOPLE WHO STEAL FROM THEIR TOMBS. SOME EGYPTIAN TOMBS HAVE CURSES ON THEIR WALLS TO SCARE OFF ROBBERS!

CURSE ON A TOMB

A tomb robber took 3 bags from a mummy's tomb. Each bag had 8 gold coins inside. How many gold coins did the robber steal in all?

Because each bag has the same number of coins, you can solve, or answer, this question using multiplication.

? bags x ? coins in each = ? coins in all

Fill in the missing numbers and solve the multiplication sentence.

POWDERED MUMMY

Many Egyptian tombs are missing their mummies. People used to steal mummies and grind them into powder for **medicine**! Sometimes, multiplication problems are missing a number. Your mummies can help!

MONSTER FACTS!

EGYPTIAN MUMMIES WERE ALSO GROUND UP TO COLOR PAINT!

There are 2 groups of mummies. They contain an equal number of mummies. There are 16 mummies total. How many mummies are in each group?

$$2 \times ? = 16$$

What number multiplied by 2, or doubled, equals 16? Try to solve the problem in your head.

MONSTROUS MUMMY TIPS

Imagine you're in a secret room in a tomb. There are 4 halls leading out. However, 5 mummies are in each hall! How many mummies in all are blocking your way?

Here's a multiplication sentence to show this problem:

$$4 \times 5 = ?$$

There's a trick to multiplying by 4: Double the other factor. Then, double that answer to find the product. So, double 5 is 10. Double 10 is 20.

$$4 \times 5 = 20$$

Use this trick to complete this multiplication sentence:

$4 \times 6 = ?$

MONSTER FACTS!

ARCHAEOLOGISTS DISCOVERED A SECRET ROOM IN THE GREAT PYRAMID IN GIZA, EGYPT, IN 2017!

A multiple is a number you get by multiplying that number by any other whole number. For example, 10 x 5 = 50, making 50 a multiple of 10.

It's easy to multiply by a two-digit number that's a multiple of 10. In fact, there's a shortcut!

Let's try this problem:

3 x 50 = ?

MONSTER FACTS!

ANCIENT EGYPTIANS EVEN MUMMIFIED CATS!

Since 50 is a multiple of 10, we can break it into two factors: 5 and 10. This means that 3 x 50 is the same as 3 x 5 x 10! Let's take a closer look at how to find the answer.

3 x 50 = 150

3 x 5 x 10 = 150

15 x 10 = 150

MUMMIES AT THE TABLE

Now that your mummy buddies have helped you understand multiplication better, you can practice **memorizing** multiplication facts. A multiplication table can help you. Use the table on the next page to solve this problem:

$$8 \times 9 = ?$$

MONSTER FACTS!

ONLY RICH EGYPTIANS COULD AFFORD THE BEST TOMBS AND THE BEST METHODS OF BEING MUMMIFIED. THE POOREST PEOPLE WERE SIMPLY BURIED IN THE DESERT AFTER THEY DIED!

	1	2	3	4	5	6	7	8	9	10
1	1	2	3	4	5	6	7	8	9	10
2	2	4	6	8	10	12	14	16	18	20
3	3	6	9	12	15	18	21	24	27	30
4	4	8	12	16	20	24	28	32	36	40
5	5	10	15	20	25	30	35	40	45	50
6	6	12	18	24	30	36	42	48	54	60
7	7	14	21	28	35	42	49	56	63	70
8	8	16	24	32	40	48	56	64	72	80
9	9	18	27	36	45	54	63	72	81	90
10	10	20	30	40	50	60	70	80	90	100

In a multiplication table, the numbers along the left column and top row are factors. The number in the square where a row and column meet is the product of the two factors.

MARVELOUS MUMMIES!

Sometimes Egyptians drew faces on the mummy's cloth wrappings or made a mask to place on the body. Then, the mummy was placed in a painted case that was set in another case. This was usually put in yet another case called a sarcophagus.

There's so much more to learn about mummies, but there's also a lot more to learn about multiplication. If you remember some of the tips from the mummies in this book, you'll be able to solve many kinds of monstrous multiplication problems!

ANCIENT EGYPTIANS BELIEVED PEOPLE NEEDED BODIES TO GO TO ANOTHER WORLD AFTER THEIR DEATH. THAT'S WHY THEY MADE MUMMIES. THEY MADE THEM SO WELL YOU CAN STILL SEE THEM IN **MUSEUMS** TODAY!

GLOSSARY

archaeologist: a scientist who studies past human life and activities

factor: an amount by which another amount is multiplied

medicine: a drug taken to make a sick person well

memorize: to learn something so that you are able to remember it perfectly

museum: a building in which things of interest are displayed

preserve: to keep something in its original state

revenge: to harm someone in return for harm done

ANSWER KEY

page 7: 35 mummies

page 9: 3 x 4 = 12 or 4 x 3 = 12; 12 mummies

page 11: 3 bags x 8 coins in each = 24 coins in all

page 13: 8 mummies

FOR MORE INFORMATION

BOOKS

Arias, Lisa. *Multiplication Meltdown*. Vero Beach, FL: Rourke Educational Media, 2015.

Hopping, Lorraine Jean. *Egyptian Mummy: Unwrap an Egyptian Mummy Layer by Layer!* Bellevue, WA: Becker & Mayer! Kids, 2017.

Lock, Deborah. *Turn to Learn Multiplication*. New York, NY: DK Publishing, 2016.

WEBSITES

How to Make a Mummy!
www.natgeokids.com/au/discover/history/egypt/how-to-make-a-mummy/
Read about the process of mummification.

Math Trainer – Multiplication
www.mathsisfun.com/numbers/math-trainer-multiply.html
Practice some multiplication problems!

Publisher's note to educators and parents: Our editors have carefully reviewed these websites to ensure that they are suitable for students. Many websites change frequently, however, and we cannot guarantee that a site's future contents will continue to meet our high standards of quality and educational value. Be advised that students should be closely supervised whenever they access the internet.

INDEX